PREHISTORIC MAN

QUESTIONS
AND
ANSWERS

Text: Juri van den Heever
Consultant: Mary Leslie
Illustrations: Ian Lusted

NEW
HOLLAND

Contents

First published in 1995 by
New Holland (Publishers) Ltd
London • Cape Town • Sydney • Singapore

Copyright © 1995 in text: Juri van den Heever
Copyright © 1995 in illustrations: Struik Image Library: Ian Lusted
Copyright © 1995 New Holland (Publishers) Ltd

ISBN 1 85368 476 7

New Holland (Publishers) Ltd
24 Nutford Place, London W1H 6DQ

Editor Susannah Coucher
Design Manager Odette Marais
Designers Darren McLean and Bettina Bard
Illustrator Ian Lusted

Typesetting by Bettina Bard
Reproduction by Unifoto (Pty) Ltd
Printed and bound by Kyodo Printing Co (Pte) Ltd, Singapore

Introduction

Most of us are interested in our family history. Finding out about our ancestors and what they did is like an exciting detective story! This book will piece together the clues. Humans have only lived on Earth for about four million years. Earlier, the land was first dominated by mammal-like reptiles and then by the dinosaurs. The mammal-like reptiles were the ancestors of the mammals which is the group we belong to. Life evolved over millions of years to produce *Homo sapiens* or modern humans. To understand all this we need to ask: What actually is a human? This is an easy question to ask but a difficult one to answer!

Can you identify these prehistoric creatures? The answers are on page 32.

What makes man?

Humans are clearly different from all other animals but if you take a closer look, you will see that we in fact share many features with animals and even a few similarities with plants! These similarities and differences can be used to group animals and plants to show how life developed on Earth. This is called classification. By studying the evolution of humans we can find out where mankind came from, who our closest relatives are and why we share so much with the other forms of life on Earth.

Are we really animals?

Yes. Humans belong to the animal kingdom because we do the things typical animals do. We move, eat, breathe and have babies. Together, these features separate all animals from plants. It is also true that amongst the animals we have a special place. Humans have the largest and most complicated brains of all animals. This is why we can invent things like computers and spaceships.

What makes us different from crabs and jellyfish?

Our bony skeleton. Because we have a bony skeleton we belong to the vertebrates or Vertebrata. This group includes the bony fish, reptiles, birds and mammals. Invertebrates like ants, snails and grasshoppers do not have a hard skeleton inside the body. Their bodies are often soft like that of a jellyfish. Some invertebrates, like snails, protect their bodies with a hard shell. Others, like crabs, form a hard cover known as a carapace.

Can humans be called mammals?

Yes. We are also classed as mammals or Mammalia together with some 4 000 other mammal species like dogs, cows and whales. Mammals range in size from tiny mice to huge elephants and whales. They are called warm-blooded because they have a constant body temperature. Their bodies are covered with fur or hair and the females produce milk to suckle the young. We are different, though, from all other mammals in the way we use complicated language to communicate with one another.

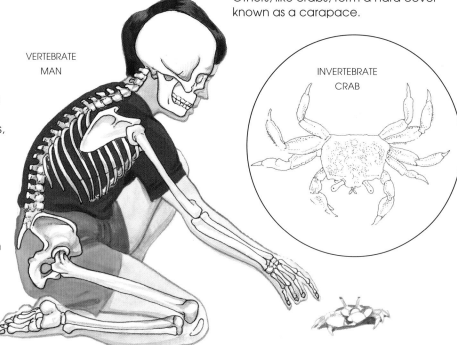

VERTEBRATE
MAN

INVERTEBRATE
CRAB

CHIMPANZEE   MAN

Are we really related to apes?

Yes. Amongst the mammals we are grouped with the primates together with about 180 species of lemurs, lorises, tarsiers, monkeys and apes. Primates generally have larger brains and good colour vision. Their eyes face forward to give '3-D' or stereoscopic vision. Primates have opposable thumbs, meaning the thumb sticks out sideways so that the hand can grasp with a power grip. The nails on the fingers and toes are flat instead of ending in claws.

ORANGUTANG

What are apes?

Chimpanzees, gorillas, orangutangs and gibbons. Apes do not have tails and their arms are longer than their legs. They have special wrist joints which are very moveable and strong. The trunk is not flattened from side to side like monkeys but shaped more like a barrel. Many primates can hold their bodies upright because they have two collar bones or clavicles which are useful for shoulder movements and for supporting the arms which can carry things.

What is a species?

A group of animals which can breed and produce fertile offspring which is fertile. Members of different species usually cannot do this. This means that all living humans belong to the same species *Homo sapiens.* Lions and tigers are one of the exceptions. They usually do not breed with each other in the wild because they live on different continents. If they are put together in a zoo they can breed and some of the offspring will be fertile.

How are we different from apes?

In many different ways. As a species we are very successful because we are the most numerous of all the large creatures on Earth and our numbers are still increasing. We have large complicated brains and walk upright on two legs. This has changed the shape of the human skeleton. The human face is flat and we have lost our fangs. We are also very clever with our hands and use complicated tools to build wonderful machines and huge buildings. One of the most amazing things about humans is the language that we use to communicate or talk to one another. Although apes also use a form of language, it seems that ours is much more complicated.

Did you know?

Humans are not less hairy than apes. We have as much or more hair on our bodies as chimpanzees or gorillas. It only looks as if we have less hair because the hairs on our bodies are smaller!

The human machine!

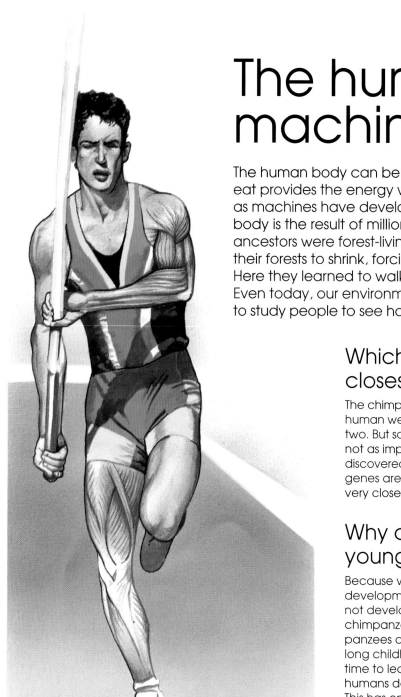

The human body can be compared to a machine. The food we eat provides the energy we need for the body to do work. Just as machines have developed over time, the modern human body is the result of millions of years of evolution. Our oldest ancestors were forest-living primates. Climatic changes caused their forests to shrink, forcing them to live on the open grasslands. Here they learned to walk upright. This is called adaptation. Even today, our environment is still changing, so it is important to study people to see how this change is affecting our bodies.

Which living ape is our closest relative?

The chimpanzee. If we looking at a chimpanzee and a human we can quickly see the differences between the two. But scientists have learnt that those differences are not as important as they once thought. They have discovered that 99 per cent of human and chimpanzee genes are similar. This means that we are genetically very closely related.

Why do humans look like young chimpanzees?

Because we are neotenous. This means that in humans, development of some features is slowed down. We do not develop long jaws and thick brow ridges like adult chimpanzees. We look much more like young chimpanzees and like them we have a long childhood. A long childhood is important because it gives us more time to learn things through experience. In this way, humans develop the ability to change their behaviour. This has enabled us to adapt more easily to changes in the environment. Neotony has therefore improved our ability to survive and has helped to make us the dominant species on Earth today.

Could we walk without our big toes?

Yes, but with difficulty. Our big toes help us to walk upright. Apes can't walk upright properly as they carry their weight on the outside edges of the feet. So they also have to use their arms for support. The human skeleton is better adapted than that of apes to walking upright. We walk by putting the weight on the heel first, then along the outer edge of the foot. The weight is then changed to the ball of the foot and we use the big toe to push off at the end of a stride.

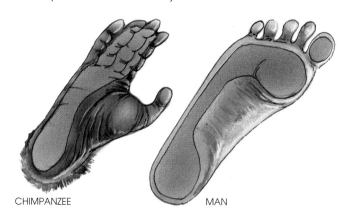

CHIMPANZEE   MAN

POWER GRIP

Do we have a grip on things?

Yes, because our thumbs are opposable. They stick out from the rest of the fingers so the hand can firmly grasp things like tools. This useful adaptation is called a power grip. If the thumb was as long as the other fingers and lay alongside them, it would be almost impossible to use tools. Looking at all the things that people have built on Earth, we can see that the power grip has been and is a very important adaptation.

Why do some people suffer from back trouble?

We're not quite used to an upright posture! Apart from headaches, back trouble is the most common cause of bodily misery! The human spine is curved like an S and carries all the weight of the upper body. In four-footed animals the spine is a simple arch and carries less weight. Most back injuries are caused by lifting, pushing, pulling and twisting. It seems as if the spine and the muscles around it have not yet adapted to the demands of modern human posture.

What does the appendix do?

Probably nothing. Humans have a portion of the intestine called an appendix. It is a small, blind-ending tube that tends to become smaller as we get older. In herbivorous mammals the appendix is very well developed and it contains bacteria which digests cellulose. Cellulose forms the walls of the cells in a plant. It seems that, as the human diet changed from plant food to include quite a lot of meat, the appendix lost its ability to digest cellulose. When it becomes infected it can be removed because it now seems to be useless. Maybe it serves to remind us of the days when we ate more plants and less meat.

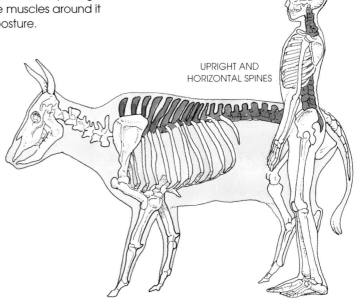

UPRIGHT AND HORIZONTAL SPINES

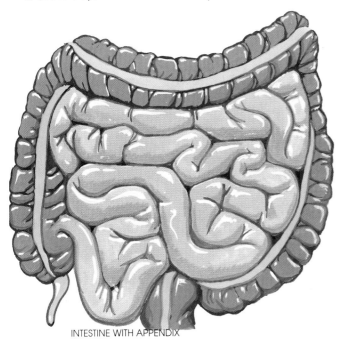

INTESTINE WITH APPENDIX

Are we the brainiest animals?

Yes. We have the largest brain of all living things. It's true that the blue whale has a larger brain than a human, but the whale is a big animal! If the weight of the brain is taken as a percentage of the body weight, then we come out tops. Even though the Neanderthal people on average had larger brains than us, our brains are more complicated than theirs and can perform many difficult tasks like building computers and doing brain surgery. Sadly, we have done silly things such as destroying the environment. We're going to have to spend time, money and effort putting it right! Because we now live in a world where brain power is important, we may succeed.

Did you know?

The adult brain is one of the largest organs in our body and weighs about 1 300 grams. It's made up of about 100 billion cells called neurons.

The living apes

The chimpanzees, gorillas, orangutangs and gibbons are our closest relatives in the animal kingdom. Apes and humans together form a Superfamily called the Hominoidea. This means that they developed from a common ancestor. Genetic studies suggest that humans and chimpanzees shared a common ancestor about eight million years ago. Chimpanzees belong to the family Pongidae and of all the primates are the most closely related to humans, but are not our direct ancestors.

Why do gibbons have such long arms?

To swing through the trees. Gibbons live in trees and move in a strange way called brachiating. Their arms are very long and their hands and feet are hook-like. This helps them to swing swiftly through the trees. Their curved fingers and opposable big toes give them a good grip, especially when they are carrying food in their arms and have to walk upright on the branches!

Where do apes hang out?

In the forests of Central Africa and South East Asia. Apes were once quite numerous in these areas but most of their living space has now been destroyed by humans. Today they survive in patches of forest which are getting smaller and smaller because the trees in which they live are cut down by loggers and the land is used for farming. These apes are also shot and eaten by humans! Often the hands of gorillas are cut off and sold as souvenirs because they are in high demand. Several of the nine species of gibbon are now on the endangered list because of the war in South East Asia.

GIBBON

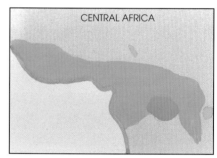

CENTRAL AFRICA

Will chimpanzees, gorillas and orangutangs survive?

Probably not. Human populations are growing too fast and need more and more space. In Africa, only 320 mountain gorillas are still alive and less than 50 000 lowland gorillas remain. Chimpanzees number fewer than 200 000.

MOUNTAIN GORILLA

Are apes knuckle walkers?

Yes, some are. This is the way most of the chimpanzees and gorillas move on the ground. They fold the fingers out of the way and support the body on the knuckles. This is called knuckle walking. Although the chimpanzees mostly live in trees, they also travel on the ground. But the gorillas are far too big to live in trees and so they do the knuckle walk!

MAP SHOWING
SOUTH EAST ASIA

CHIMPANZEE CATCHING TERMITES

Are apes handy with tools?

Yes. At the Gombe National Park in Tanzania, chimpanzees look for termites by sticking grass stalks into the termites' nests. When these termites climb onto the stalk, the chimpanzees quickly pull out the stalk and gobble up the termites! Chimpanzees will also use sticks to get at something edible that is floating in the water. In the Tai forest of the Ivory Coast chimpanzees use rocks to crack the shells of nuts.

Are chimps nut-cracking experts?

Yes! They cleverly use rocks as hammers. The nuts of the Panda tree in West Africa have very hard shells and are difficult to crack open. Chimpanzees have learnt how to solve this problem. They put the nuts carefully into knotholes in the roots of trees. The shell is then cracked open with a rock which is held in both hands. Because rocks are very scarce in the Tai forest, chimpanzees have to remember where the rock was last used. When they need the rock again, they know where to find it. This shows us that chimpanzees, like humans, have good memories!

CHIMPANZEE CRACKING NUTS

Are chimpanzees also meat-eaters?

Yes. Chimpanzees sometimes eat monkeys or other small animals. In West Africa they even hunt in a group. A few chimpanzees will wait in the trees while one will chase the monkey into the ambush. The meat is then shared.

Why do chimps go to all this trouble to be nutcrackers?

Because nuts are very nutritious food. By eating nuts a chimpanzee gets all the nourishment it needs, without having to look for any other food. By only eating leaves, a chimpanzee would have to spend much more time looking for food because leaves are less nourishing than nuts. Nutcracking is an important learned skill because it helps the chimpanzees to survive. Just like human mothers, chimpanzees teach their children exactly how to crack these nuts so that they will survive in the forests and will later pass on this valuable skill to their children.

RED COLOBUS MONKEY

Hunting for our fossil ancestors

Fossils provide important information about the history of life on Earth. They are usually found in rock layers formed from mud or sand. These are known as sedimentary rocks and form a large portion of the surface of the Earth. Each fossil tells us about a particular time in the past and is usually found with the animals and plants of that time. Because animals and plants can tell us about the climate, these fossils are very important in helping us to reconstruct the prehistoric environment of our ancestors.

FOSSIL SKULL AND TOOLS

What are fossils?

Any evidence that life existed in the past. The best fossils of prehistoric humans are their petrified teeth and bones. Bone is the hardest tissue in the human body and so is the most easily preserved. Fossil footprints of prehistoric humans that have been discovered give us fascinating clues as to when they started to walk upright. The tools early people used, the charred bones of the prey they hunted and the shells they collected are fossil evidence of their way of life.

How do things become fossils?

It is not easy to become a fossil! When something dies it is usually eaten by scavengers. In this way, the bones are widely spread about. That is why the fossils of complete skeletons are hardly ever found. For the bones to become fossilised they must be covered with mud or clay before they are destroyed by weathering. So, most fossils that are found will be in the sedimentary rocks that form around lakes or on the floodplains between rivers. As the mud or clay hardens into rock the bones are preserved by minerals which replace the original bone material. If the rocks are exposed to the weather, they are worn down and eventually the fossils are seen and can be collected.

Who discovers fossils?

Palaeontologists and their helpers. Palaeoanthropologists study prehistoric man. Because it's important to know about early man's ancient environment, help from other scientists is needed. Geologists map the fossil site and study the rock layers while the palaeobotanists study the plant fossils. Palaeozoologists will study the animal remains and the palaeoclimatologists will then study the ancient climate. When all this information is put together it'll show scientists what the prehistoric environment was like.

How can we tell how old a fossil is?

In different ways. In nature, the older rock layers are found lower down in the Earth so the fossils from the lower layers will be the oldest. This is not a very precise method. With other, more precise methods, the rock in which the fossil is found is analysed to find out its age. The potassium/argon or K/Ar method is the best known and is used on volcanic rock. Scientists compare the amount of argon or gas in a rock sample with the amount of potassium in the original rock to work out how old the fossil is.

Why are there so few hominid fossils?

Hominids formed only a small part of prehistoric life. Many lived in areas where fossils did not form easily. The hominid fossils that have been found are often the remains of prey which have been eaten by carnivores. After prehistoric man started using fire, these fossils became fewer in number. Fire would have been useful for protection and may have been used to chase carnivores out of the caves so that hominids could live there themselves.

Can we find out how prehistoric man lived?

Yes. Often the shape and size of their teeth and the way in which they are worn give us a good idea of what our ancestors ate. The bones of animals that have been found with human fossils show us which animals lived at that particular time. We can tell how food was prepared by looking at the way in which the bones have been broken and whether or not the bones were cooked in a fire. The tools or the weapons found with the fossils show what kinds of things they made. At one site in Germany, a large, sharpened wooden spear which was about three metres long was found between the fossilised ribs of an elephant. This suggests that some ancient Neanderthal hunter probably defended himself or killed the elephant during a hunt.

ATTACKING AN ELEPHANT

RECONSTRUCTING
A SKULL

What did our early ancestors look like?

They didn't look very different from us. When they study a fossil skull, scientists can actually see where the muscles were attached to the bone. The muscles are then modelled in clay and put back on the skull in the correct positions. The shape of the nose and lips and the colour of the eyes can only be guessed. Finally, the fat and connective tissue just under the skin are added. Towards the end when the skin is modelled, we will be able to see an incredibly accurate three-dimensional reconstruction of a prehistoric human skull!

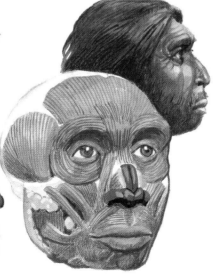

11

Our primate ancestors

The first mammals evolved about 200 million years ago when dinosaurs still ruled the Earth. They were the size of mice and for millions of years afterwards mammals weren't very prominent on land. About 65 million years ago, at the end of the Cretaceous Period, changes in the Earth's climate killed off the last dinosaurs. The mammals survived and filled the gap left by the dinosaurs to eventually take over the Earth. Their numbers increased dramatically and many different kinds developed. This is called adaptive radiation. Among the first mammal groups to develop were the primates. They looked very different from the primates of today but from this small beginning rose the human family.

Where on Earth did the first primates appear?

We are not sure. Some scientists think that they evolved in Africa even before the dinosaurs became extinct, but the fossil record of Africa at that time is too disjointed to be sure. From about 65 to 58 million years ago fossils of the early primates became more common and they are found in North America and Europe. Several different groups of primates then developed. About 36 million years ago lemurs and bushbabies had appeared as well as the Old World monkeys of Europe, Africa and Asia and the New World monkeys of North and South America. Today lemurs are only found in Madagascar.

PLESIADAPIS

What did the first primates look like?

Probably a bit like squirrels. One of the best examples is *Plesiadapis*. It lived about 57 million years ago. Like squirrels, the earliest primates lived in trees as well as on the forest floor. They had claws instead of nails like later primates. Their rather large front teeth were still specialised for cracking open the hard bodies of insects. Their chewing teeth looked more like those of the later primates and show us that their diet had changed to include more plant food.

DISTRIBUTION OF MODERN PRIMATES

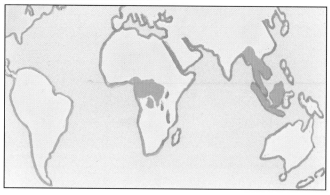

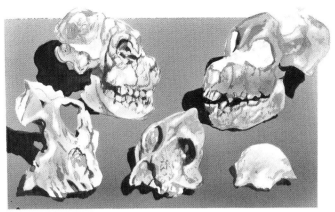
AEGYPTOPITHECUS SKULLS

Why were forests a good place to live?

There was food and shelter. Flowering plants developed during the Cretaceous Period. Towards the end of this period, huge forests had spread widely on Earth. With the increase of the flowering plants the insects also multiplied. This is why the first primates lived in forests and developed special teeth so that they could eat insects. Life in the trees meant that primates had to jump carefully from branch to branch. That is probably why they developed grasping hands with opposable thumbs and forward-looking eyes with 3-D vision.

What is the Fayum Depression?

A rich fossil site in Egypt at the edge of the Sahara desert. About thirty million years ago this was a lush forest with rivers that flowed into the Mediterranean sea. The oldest primate fossils in Africa were found here. One of them was a monkey-like creature known as *Aegyptopithecus*. It was the size of a big house cat with small eyes, a sign that it was active during the day. Some scientists think that *Aegyptopithecus* may have been the ancestor of both modern apes and people.

Why is *Proconsul* a very important ape?

It was probably also a common ancestor of apes and humans. *Proconsul* lived in Africa about 18 million years ago. It looked a lot like a modern chimpanzee but all four of its limbs were about the same length. A chimpanzee's arms are longer than its legs. *Proconsul's* eyes faced forward for 3-D vision and the brain was quite large. Its molar teeth were adapted to eat fruit. *Proconsul* had no special adaptations for leaping or swinging in the trees or walking on the ground. It also seems to have walked on its palms and not on its knuckles. Because of these and other adaptations some scientists are convinced that *Proconsul* may have been the common ancestor of both todays' humans and the great apes.

PROCONSUL

GORILLA SKULL

GIGANTOPITHECUS SKULL

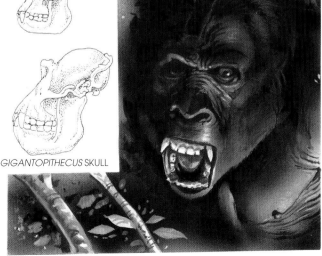

Were there really giants among the apes?

Yes. *Gigantopithecus* was enormous and lived during the last part of the Miocene up to about 500 000 years ago. It stood over two metres tall and weighed up to 300 kilograms. It may have been the largest primate that ever lived. It was first discovered in medicine shops in China where the teeth, known as 'dragon's teeth,' were sold as medicine. Many stories are told about *Gigantopithecus* and some people even think that it may have survived long enough in small groups to give rise to the legend of the Abominable Snowman. It may have been a frightening creature but it probably lived on bamboo shoots!

Our earliest hominid ancestors

About seven million years ago the climate in Africa started changing. It became drier and in many parts, forests were slowly replaced by open grassland or savannah. Such changes affect the ecology and can put so much stress on animals and plants that some may die out. Other plants and animals are often able to change and adapt to the new environment. In this way, new species can be formed. From about eight to five million years ago, the human fossil record is poor but we do know that at about five million years ago a new creature appeared in Africa. It still had a small brain but walked upright on two legs much like we do. It adapted to life on the open grassland and was our earliest human ancestor. Scientists have named this creature *Australopithecus* or the southern ape.

Who is Lucy?

The most complete *Australopithecus* fossil yet found. Lucy was found at Hadar in northern Ethiopia in 1974. The shape of the hip bone and the birth canal shows that she was almost certainly female. The length of the femur or thigh bone shows that she was about one metre tall and the weight bearing area of the hip socket shows that she weighed about 27 kilograms. She was an adult because her wisdom teeth had already grown through and show some wear. Pieces of the braincase show that her brain was about one quarter the size of a modern human brain.

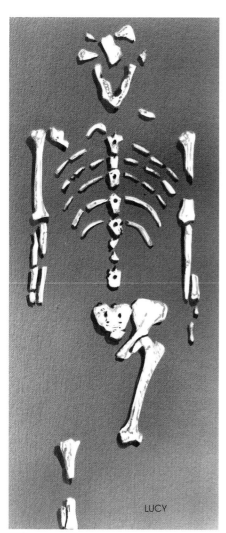

LUCY

What happened at Laetoli?

Somebody left human footprints in a layer of volcanic ash. About 3.5 million years ago the volcano Sadiman in northern Tanzania blew out clouds of volcanic ash which covered the landscape. Shortly afterwards it rained and three prehistoric humans walked over the wet ash leaving very clear footprints. The footprints then hardened. These tracks are very important because they confirm that the first austrolopithecines walked upright like we do.

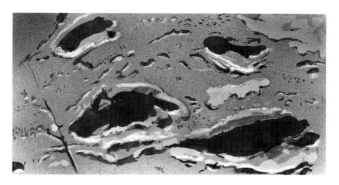

LAETOLI FOOTPRINTS

Which was the first *Australopithecus* fossil discovered?

The Taung child. The word, 'Taung' means 'Place of the Lion' and is the site of an old lime mine near Kimberley in South Africa. In 1925, Dr Raymond Dart described the fossilised skull of a young child from Taung as a human ancestor and called it *Australopithecus africanus*. This first find caused a worldwide stir. More fossils have been found at Sterkfontein, Swartkrans and Kromdraai near Krugersdorp and Makapansgat near Pietersburg in South Africa. Some are similar to the Taung child. Others have heavier jaw and skull bones and are called *Australopithecus robustus* or *Paranthropus*.

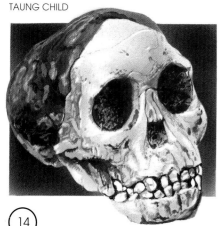

TAUNG CHILD

Was *Australopithecus* a killer-ape?

No. At first, scientists thought that *Australopithecus* was a hunter because of the way the animal bones (which were found amongst them) were broken. Today we know that these bones are probably the leftovers of meals of carnivores like leopards and sabre-tooth cats and scavengers like hyaenas and porcupines. The teeth of *Australopithecus africanus* show that it was a herbivore and mainly ate plants. Fine scratches on the teeth look like those of animals that eat fruit and leaves. There is no good evidence to show that they regularly ate meat but they may sometimes have caught and eaten small vertebrates. The very large back teeth of *Paranthropus* are worn in a different way. It probably liked to eat the tough, gritty bulbs and tubers of plants that grew in the hard soil and had to be dug out of the ground.

Did *Australopithecus* use tools?

Probably. Scientists aren't certain. There is no evidence that *Australopithecus* could make stone tools like the hominids that came after them. Some of the fossilised horn cores (the bony prongs inside animal horns) found with *Paranthropus*, have polished areas as if somebody had been digging in the ground with them. The teeth of *Paranthropus* show that it probably ate tough, gritty food like bulbs and tubers and it seems likely that they used bits of broken bone to dig out the bulbs and tubers. So although *Paranthropus* may not have been a regular toolmaker it probably was a tool user.

PARANTHROPUS

Did *Australopithecus* have any enemies?

Yes. We know that *Paranthropus* was caught and eaten by leopards. Some of the fossil skulls found at Swartkrans in South Africa show bite marks that match the fangs of fossil leopard skulls also found at Swartkrans. Leopards often take their prey up into a tree for safekeeping. Even today trees still grow at the entrance to underground caves like Swartkrans. It is likely that many of the fossils found at Swartkrans were in fact leopard prey that had dropped into the cave from the trees above.

Did you know?

Walking upright actually helps to prevent overheating. When our ancestors left the forests they had to live on the open grasslands. Moving about in the direct tropical sunlight on all fours would have made the heat unbearable. One way to adapt is to walk upright so the vertical rays of the overhead Sun fall mainly on the head and shoulders. The rest of the body would then stay cooler and so help prevent overheating. This explains why we have lots of hair protecting our heads and why we have small hairs on the rest of the body to help with cooling.

Handy Man, the first toolmaker

MODERN MAN AND HANDY MAN

About 2.5 million years ago the first stone tools appeared in Africa. Similar tools were first noticed at Olduvai Gorge, a famous fossil site in Tanzania. They were called the Oldowan. These simply-made tools were found with the remains of a more advanced hominid who was thought to have been the toolmaker. They called it *Homo habilis* or the Handy Man. Fragments of braincase showed that this hominid had a larger brain than *Australopithecus.* Scientists believe that there is a link between larger brains and the skill of tool making.

What did Handy Man look like?

A lot like *Australopithecus. Homo habilis* was about 1.2 metres tall and weighed about 40 kilograms. Their skeletons show that they walked and stood more or less upright. Because they had larger brains their skulls looked different. The forehead bulged more at the front. This made the face look flatter but not as flat as that of the modern humans. The teeth, especially the canines or eye teeth, were smaller than those of *Australopithecus* and more like those of modern people. The wear marks on the teeth show that *Homo habilis* was an omnivore and ate both meat and plants.

What tools do we find in the first human tool kit?

Core tools and flake tools. First a suitable pebble was selected. Using another stone as a hammer, pieces were struck off to give the pebble a sharp cutting edge. The remains of the pebble is called the core and the thin pieces that were struck off the sides are called flakes. The flakes were important bits because they had very sharp edges. These simple tools were made by our ancestors for about a million years.

MAKING EARLY TOOLS

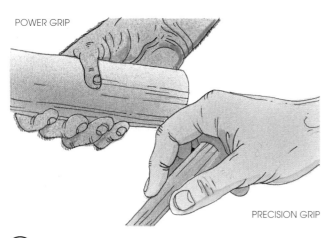

POWER GRIP

PRECISION GRIP

Was *Homo habilis* really handy?

Yes. Like apes we can hold tools between our thumbs and fingers in a power grip. People also have strong thumbs with special muscles to help them hold things firmly between the thumb and the fingers. This is called a precision grip. The apes do not have these thumb muscles. To work with tools, especially small tools, the precision grip must be used. Fossils show that Handy Man probably had special thumb muscles like ours and was able to make and use tools just like us.

What were the tools used for?

Probably mostly for obtaining food. Some flakes were used as scrapers to scrape or saw wood. Others may have been used to cut grass or reeds. Some were used to cut meat because the bones of the animals found with them show cut marks made by the tools. The larger cores may also have been used for rough butchering and for cracking open bones to get at the marrow which was probably popular with early man.

Was *Homo habilis* a hunter?

Perhaps, but plant foods made up most of their diet. They probably collected small animals and insects and seem to have eaten more meat than *Australopithecus*. Most of the meat they ate was probably scavenged or stolen. Paleoanthropologists are studying the bones and stones preserved at these very old sites, hoping to find some clues.

Did *Homo habilis* go camping?

Yes. At Olduvai there are areas where the ground is littered with tools, bones and horns. These living areas were usually near a stream or a lake. At these sites, tools are mixed with animal bones that were broken and crushed before being fossilised. At some places the bones are sorted into different piles, one pile containing marrow bones and the other without any marrow bones at all.

Dia *Homo habilis* build shelters?

We don't really know for sure. At one Olduvai site a rough, indistinct circle of stones was found. The circle is made of blocks of lava and is about four metres across. At first, scientists thought it was the base of a shelter built from branches. Now many think that this structure may have actually formed quite naturally. Similar stone circles are found where tree roots break up the lava rock.

Out of Africa: The first explorers

About 1.8 million years ago *Homo erectus* or upright man. appeared on Earth. He evolved in Africa and lived there for more than a million years. At first *Homo erectus* lived only in Africa but very soon he migrated from Africa to the Near East and South East Asia. These were the first of the hominids to leave the warm African climate and live in cooler areas. It seems that they could do this because they were well adapted to walking on two legs. They had bigger brains and better tools than earlier hominids which helped them become so successful.

Who was Java Man?

The first *Homo erectus* fossil ever found. Mr Eugene Dubois, a Dutch anatomist, thought that the fossil ancestors of modern humans would be found in Asia. He left Amsterdam as an army doctor to search for this 'missing link' in the East. In 1891 he discovered part of a human skull and a thigh bone on the island of Java. He named his fossil *Pithecanthropus erectus*. Java man seemed so similar to us that it was renamed *Homo erectus*.

Who was Peking man?

Fossils of *Homo erectus* found in China. Between 1921 and 1937 at the village of Zhoukoudian near Beijing, then called Peking, fossil fragments of about 40 men, women and children were found. They were named *Sinanthropus pekinensis* or Chinese Man of Peking. When scientists later decided that Peking Man and Java Man were similar and probably our direct ancestors, the name was changed to *Homo erectus*.

Could *Homo erectus* talk?

We do not know. We use our larynx to talk. The larynx sits lower in our throats than in apes. Apes can't make the complicated sounds that we do. In fossils of *Homo erectus* the larynx was located lower in the throat than in the apes but not as low as in modern people. This means that *Homo erectus* probably did have the beginnings of true speech.

LARYNX IN *HOMO ERECTUS* AND MODERN MAN

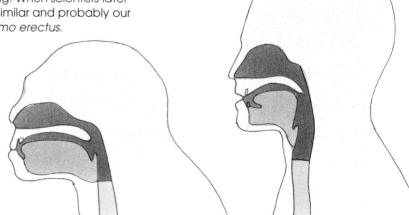

Why is the Boy from Turkana a hot issue?

Because it is the most complete *Homo erectus* ever found. About 1.6 million years ago a boy of 12 died in a marsh near Lake Turkana in Kenya. The skeleton is almost complete because the body was covered and preserved in mud before scavengers could tear it apart. At death he was already 157 centimetres tall and weighed about 50 kilograms. His height shows that he was adapted to a hot, dry environment. He also walked and moved just like us. Some scientists think that the Turkana Boy and other early *Homo erectus* fossils deserve a separate name, *Homo ergaster* or Working Man.

Who invented the Handaxe?

Homo erectus. Many years ago (about one and a half million years ago) a new stone industry, we call the Acheulean, appeared in Africa. The typical stone tools are called bifaces. The cutting edges were flaked carefully on both sides. The tools were usually fifteen to thirty centimetres long. Some are pointed and so are called handaxes. A few have broad cutting edges and are called cleavers. Others are thick and are called picks. The shapes are so standard that we think the toolmakers had a particular pattern in mind. This may in fact mean that the brain of *Homo erectus* was probably better organised than that of *Homo habilis*.

HANDAXE

BOY FROM TURKANA

Did you know?

The fossils of Peking Man which were found near the village of Zhoukoudian are all lost. When the Second World War broke out Japan invaded China. To keep the fossils safe it was decided to send them to North America. The fossils were smuggled out of Beijing but unfortunately the soldiers guarding them were captured and the fossils vanished without a trace. To this day, nobody has been able to find them again. Fortunately plaster casts were made of the original fossils so today scientists work with these!

Was *Homo erectus* the first firemaker?

Yes. The cave at Zhoukoudian in China, where the winters were cold, contains layers of ash and charcoal which shows that *Homo erectus* used fire in the cave about 500 000 years ago. The African *Homo erectus* may have been using fire much earlier. In Kenya burnt patches of clay found at some sites show where fires may have been made about 1.4 million years ago. At the Swartkrans cave in South Africa, burnt pieces of bone show that *Homo erectus* may also have been cooking his food about a million years ago.

WHERE MAN FIRST MADE FIRE

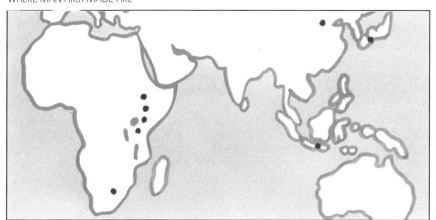

The first wise men

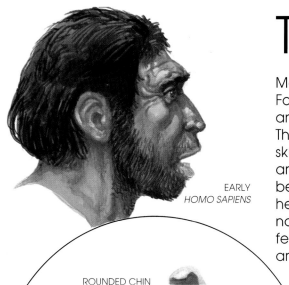

EARLY
HOMO SAPIENS

Modern people are called *Homo sapiens* or Man the Wise. Fossils of the earliest *Homo sapiens* are found in Africa, Europe and Asia. They lived from about 500 000 to 130 000 years ago. Their skeletons looked a lot like those of *Homo erectus* but their skulls were different because they had a larger brain. These archaic or early *Homo sapiens* did not look quite like us either because they still had a bony ridge above the eyes, a low forehead and large jaws and teeth. They also had a rounded chin, not like the pointy ones which we have! Because of these differences scientists have given us a slightly different name. We are called *Homo sapiens sapiens*.

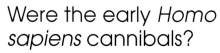

ROUNDED CHIN

Do bigger brains really make better tools?

Eventually. About 200 000 years ago archaic *Homo sapiens* developed another way to make tools. This is called the prepared-core technique. The core was carefully prepared by striking off flakes to give it the right shape. Then the toolmaker could strike off just one flake of exactly the size or shape that was wanted. In Europe, a popular prepared-core shape which we call Levallois produced the triangular points typical of the Mousterian.

Were the early *Homo sapiens* cannibals?

Probably. A skull from Arago in south western France, found amongst fragments of animal bones, has the back part broken away. Skulls from Ngandong in Java have the undersides broken out. It seems that these skulls were deliberately opened to get at the brains. A skull from Bodo in Ethiopia has cut marks in the eye sockets. Scientists think that these marks were made by tools used to cut the flesh off the skull after death.

Who suffered from toothache?

The young man from Kabwe in Zambia. This archaic *Homo sapiens* skull also known as Broken Hill Man, has very badly decayed teeth. Parts of the upper jaw were actually eaten away by tooth abscesses before he died. Fossil skulls nearly always have good teeth because the food our ancestors ate contained very little sugar. Why Kabwe Man had such bad teeth more than 300 000 years ago still remains a mystery. A possible explanation is that he was just a little too fond of wild honey.

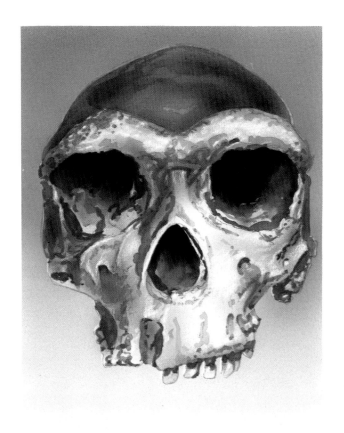

KABWE SKULL

Did early *Homo sapiens* ever use wooden tools?

Yes. They probably used bits of wood as tools long before this but nothing has been preserved. The best direct evidence that wood was used at this time to make tools is a spear point found at Clacton in England. It is made from the wood of a yew tree and is 300 000 years old.

Did they use fire?

Yes. At most sites there is evidence of fire. It seems that early *Homo sapiens* regularly used and controlled fire. Pieces of burnt bone found in shallow depressions show where camp fires were made. Because of the way in which these bones were changed by the heat, scientists know that they were put into a fire and not accidentally charred in a natural bush fire.

Did they live in shelters?

Perhaps. Early *Homo sapiens* still lived in caves and open air camp sites. By about 400 000 years ago they may have been building huts. At Terra Amata above the bay of Nice in south eastern France, collections of stones were found. The excavator thought that they supported a hut made from sticks stuck in the ground and bent together at the top. The hut would have been about seven and a half metres long and about four metres wide. Some scientists do not think the evidence we have supports this interpretation. Only time will tell.

Were early *Homo sapiens* big game hunters?

Probably not. At Terra Amata these *Homo sapiens* left behind the bones of elephant, wild boar, deer and rabbits. Scientists think it is unlikely that they could kill bigger game like elephants with the weapons they had. They may have cut pieces off large dead animals they found and took them back to their camp site. They could have also hunted the young of these animals because their small bones are found at the site. They were probably also very good at hunting smaller game.

Hunters of the Ice Age

Between 200 000 and 150 000 years ago a specialised human group appeared in Europe and western Asia! These people are called Neanderthals, after a fossil site in the Neander Valley near Dusseldorf in Germany. 'Typical' Neanderthalers lived from about 90 000 to 35 000 years ago. Their heads were different from ours. The skull was long and flat with a big bump at the back. As they were like us in many other ways it was thought that they were the direct ancestors of living people. Today, we think that this is not true. At the same time that the Neanderthals lived in Europe and western Asia other, more modern people lived in Africa and the Far East. Scientists think now that the Africans, not the Neanderthals, are the most likely direct ancestors of living humans!

What is an 'Ice Age'?

An extremely cold period of time. Over the last 1.7 million years the climate of the Earth has changed several times from warm to cold and back again. The warm periods are known as interglacials. The Neanderthal people lived during a cold period or 'Ice Age'. At that time the ice cap at the North Pole spread southwards and grew so large that it covered much of Europe, Asia and North America. Today we live in yet another interglacial.

NEANDERTHAL MAN

What did the Neanderthals look like?

They were shorter than modern people but stockily built. An adult was about 150 centimetres tall (shoulder height of a modern person) and weighed about 70 kilograms. They had strong thick bones and short legs. Compared with us, Neanderthals had low foreheads and large faces with broad noses. Above the eyes there was still a well developed bony ridge. A large nose is an adaptation to a cold climate because the cold air inhaled through the nose is warmed before it reaches the sensitive lungs. The same feature can be seen in people such as the Eskimos who also live in a very cold climate.

MAP OF AN ICE AGE

Did the Neanderthals walk like us?

Yes. In 1908 a Neanderthal fossil called the 'Old man of La Chapelle' was found in France. The skeleton belonged to an old man who had suffered from arthritis. When the deformed bones were first described it was thought that they belonged to a stooped person who walked with bent knees, dragging his feet. Later, when it was restudied and other skeletons had been found scientists realised that the Neanderthals walked exactly like us.

Why did the Neanderthals have worn front teeth?

Probably because they used their teeth to prepare animal hides for clothes. Scientists think that the Neanderthals used their front teeth to grip hides while scraping bits of flesh and other tissues from the inside surface. A typical feature of Neanderthal teeth is that the front surface of the incisors or front teeth are worn away. This kind of wear does not come from chewing food, but from gripping something between the teeth.

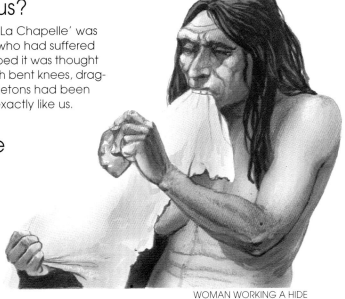

WOMAN WORKING A HIDE

CAVE BEAR

Did they worship the great cave bear?

No. The enormous cave bear *Ursus spelaeus* lived at the same time as the Neanderthals. At Drachenloch (Dragon cave) in Switzerland, skulls and bones of cave bears were found along the walls of the cave. At first it was thought that the bones were specially placed in the caves and worshipped by the Neanderthals. This gave rise to the popular idea of a Neanderthal 'Cult of the Cave Bear.' Some scientists think that these fossils came from bears that died naturally or hibernated (slept during winter) in the caves.

Did they bury their dead?

Yes. Neanderthals were the first people to bury their dead regularly. Some scientists think that they did it just so that scavengers could not get at the corpses. Others think that Neaderthal people held funeral ceremonies. At the Shanidar cave in Iraq a Neanderthal grave was found containing lots of pollen from different flowers. This could mean that the corpse was laid to rest with a 'flower ceremony'. As there is also evidence of burrowing rodents at the grave, some scientists think that the pollen came from the rodents' plant food.

What was Neanderthal life like?

Neanderthal people lived in small groups, hunting for meat and collecting plant food. They made wooden spears and beautiful knives, spearheads, scrapers, and borers from stone. Their tools are called Mousterian after the Le Moustier cave in France. They knew how to make and use fire because burnt bones are found at many sites. They probably roasted animals like deer, bison, wild ox, cave bear, and even mammoth and woolly rhinoceros. The last Neanderthals living in western Europe were replaced by more modern people moving in.

NEANDERTHAL BURIAL

The appearance of modern people

One of the last steps in our evolution was the appearance of *Homo sapiens sapiens*. The earliest of these people are called anatomically modern humans because they looked almost exactly like us but lived more than 100 000 years ago. Their skeletons were similar to those of *Homo erectus* except above the neck. The skull was larger and more lightly built. The face was smaller and the forehead upright with the brow ridges small or absent. They had pointy chins like us! The appearance of anatomically modern people on Earth was an important event in human evolution but it is still not well understood. *Homo sapiens sapiens* eventually spread far and wide and came to live in all the habitable regions of the world.

HOMO SAPIENS SAPIENS

Where did these humans first live?

In Africa, south of the Sahara. The best evidence for the oldest anatomically modern people comes from Klasies River in South Africa. Here several modern jaw fragments date between 120 000 and 60 000 years old. Similar fossils from Border Cave near Swaziland are about 90 000 years old. There are also other fossils from Florisbad in South Africa, Laetoli in Tanzania and Omo in Ethiopia which are less well dated. These early modern fossils support the 'Out of Africa' theory. This is the idea that the ancestors of modern people lived in Africa more than 100 000 years ago and then spread to Europe and the Far East.

SITES OF EARLIEST *HOMO SAPIENS SAPIENS*

Did they build shelters?

Perhaps. They often lived in caves like Klasies River, but also on open sites. If they built shelters we would be lucky to find any evidence. Shelters of wood and animal skins don't last well. We do have some mammoth bone shelters from about 15 000 years ago. These huts were built on the plains of Eastern Europe and had fireplaces inside. The walls of one hut were supported on the outside by 95 mammoth lower jaws carefully stacked around the base.

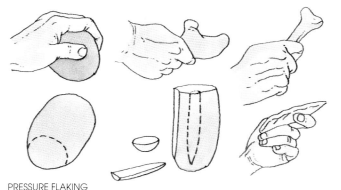
PRESSURE FLAKING

Were they expert toolmakers?

Yes. The modern people who replaced the Neanderthals in western Europe are famous for their culture which we call the Upper Paleolithic. They made stone tools which were pressure flaked with soft bone hammers. They used lots of red ochre. They painted pictures on the walls of their caves. Sea shells, animal teeth and carved bone and ivory were used to decorate themselves. They made clay and bone figurines and carved bone tools. The Upper Paleolithic sites of western Europe are well known. As we find more sites we see that these 'modern' skills were widespread in other parts of the world.

How did they reach America?

They walked across from Asia. The first people to reach America were anatomically modern. They probably arrived some time after the last glacial maximum. This was about 18 000 years ago. At that time there was so much ice at the Poles that the sea level was much lower than it is today. Asia and North America were connected by a wide strip of land called Beringia. Today, it is covered by water and called the Bering Straits. In those days animals would have been able to walk from one continent to another and they would have been followed by the hunters and their families. Eventually people moved all the way down to South America.

When did they reach Australia?

Probably between 50 000 and 40 000 years ago from South East Asia. The sea level would have been about 400 feet lower then. There would still have been at least 60 miles of ocean to cross. Boats and some understanding of navigation would have been needed! There are not a lot of early fossils from Australia. They are very interesting but not very well understood.

SPEAR THROWER

Did you know?

Spear-throwers were used in southern France about 14 000 years ago. They were made out of wood or bone with a hook at one end. The back end of the spear was fitted into the hook and the hunter gripped the front end of the spear-thrower. Spears used like this can be thrown much harder and further to kill a wider variety of animals.

PELOROVIS

Why did the giant buffalo die out?

Probably because of the way they were hunted. *Pelorovis*, the giant buffalo of southern Africa was so large that it would have been very dangerous to hunt. At one site it has been shown that the bones of these beasts were nearly all adults or newly-born calves. Scientists think that the hunters waited until the cows were giving birth before killing them. This would have been safer. This practice of killing the females when they were giving birth could have caused the giant buffalo to become extinct.

The first farmers

Modern humans gradually spread around the world. They moved around a lot, hunting animals for meat and collecting other foods like bulbs, fruits and seeds. Later they lived in permanent villages and produced their own food. The women tended fields of grain and the men tamed animals to use as livestock. When pottery was invented, grain could be stored in great jars of baked clay. Scientists agree that farming first started in the Middle East. It changed the world because it meant that more and more people could live on small areas of fertile land. It was as important an event as learning to make tools and use fire. Our modern civilization started with these farming villages. Unfortunately, it was also the first step towards the population explosion and the pollution of the environment.

HARVESTING GRAIN

Who baked the first bread?

Nobody really knows. At first people didn't bake bread. The grain kernels were crushed with a grindstone and then dried over a fire. The dried grain was mixed with water to make a crunchy porridge. In ancient Egypt women baked bread. Scientists have found that the bread contained sand. It was blown into the dough by the wind since Egyptian women cooked outdoors.

What is the fertile crescent?

The area in the Near East where farming was first started. About 10 000 years ago people learnt how to sow and harvest the wheat that grew wild in this area. They were fortunate that the climate on the grassy hills of the fertile crescent was just right to grow wheat. This meant that for the first time they could settle in one place and produce their own food. When people began to grow their own food they built permanent villages to live in. These villages gradually grew larger and larger and became the towns and cities of modern times.

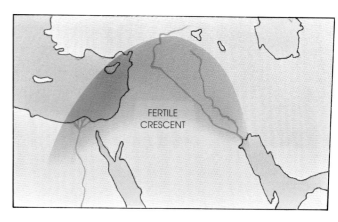

FERTILE CRESCENT

Did people start farming in other places too?

Yes. Farming was invented in several different places around the world. About 8 000 years ago people in Mexico were growing squash and beans. In China, people were farming with grain called millet 6 000 years ago. Farming did not immediately take over from the hunter and gatherer lifestyle. Hunter-gatherers were very successful and in some parts of the world like Australia, they still manage to survive in this way.

Where do dogs come from?

They were bred from wolves. Wolves were the first animals tamed by humans about 20 000 years ago. Wolves eat just about anything and were probably tamed when they scavenged the rotting carcasses at camp sites of hunters. In this way they also kept the humans healthy because the carcasses attracted flies that spread diseases. Dogs still do this today.

What was the first farm tool?

Probably the sickle. About 12 000 years ago people in the Middle East were using sickles to harvest wild grain like wheat and barley. These sickles were made out of wood or bone with a groove at the front. Small, very sharp pieces of stone called flint were fitted into the groove and fixed in place with pine resin. The flint blades gave the sickle a very sharp cutting edge and made the harvesting of grain much easier.

ANCIENT SICKLE

Who invented the plough?

The Egyptians. About 7 000 years ago Egyptians were active farmers. While most of the rest of the world were still hunter-gatherers they ploughed their fields with a stick plough pulled by domesticated cattle.

Where do farm animals come from?

From herds of wild sheep, goats and cattle. The first farm animals were sheep, tamed by people of the Near East between 10 000 and 11 000 years ago. At first they would have been hunted but then they may have been driven into places where they could be penned until needed for food. The young would then have grown up close to people and become tame to form the first herds of livestock.

Prehistoric art and artists

Most people are fond of listening to music and looking at paintings and sculptures. Art is an important part of our culture and it separates us from the animals. In the past it was different because for hundreds of thousands of years our ancestors did not seem to have the capacity for art. About 35 000 years ago people started painting and scratching images of the animals they knew on the walls of their caves. Many of these paintings are very beautiful and can still be clearly seen today. The first musical instruments also appeared during this time as well as small carved statues and jewellery made out of bone or ivory. For the first time in history, humans were not just making tools but also things that were beautiful to look at. This was the very beginning of our culture.

Who painted the caves of Europe?

Modern people of the Upper Paleolithic. Neanderthal people left us very little evidence of art. At some Neanderthal sites coloured pigments were found but some scientists think that they used these pigments to decorate their bodies. At a Neanderthal site in Hungary a pebble has been found with a cross scratched on it. The later Upper Paleolithic people painted their cave walls and made clay figurines and engraved their bone tools.

How could they work in the dark European caves?

They used lamps that burned animal fat. The artists worked deep in the caves. They used small cuplike lamps of hollow stone, sea shells or bowls made from skulls. These were filled with animal fat and set alight. Locks of hair or pieces of dried moss served as wicks. The artists probably did not live so deep inside the caves. The position of the paintings may show they had special or religious meaning. The paintings in the deep European caves have survived for at least 35 000 years. Similar traditions in Australia and Southern Africa may be as old or older. At Apollo 11, in Namibia, painted slabs have been dated to about 27 000 years.

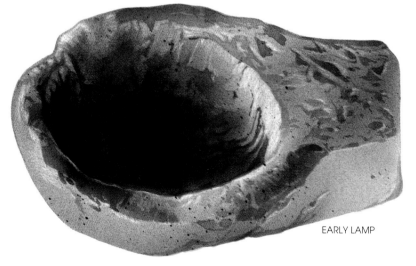

EARLY LAMP

What did they use to paint with?

Mineral pigments called haematite, limonite and manganese. These pigments are found near the caves where the paintings were made. Manganese is usually black but can often be purplish. Limonite can vary from yellow through red to dark brown. Haematite is red or ochre coloured.

Did they use paint brushes?

Not always. It seems that some of the paintings were done with the tips of the fingers. Sometimes they blew paint onto the wall through a bone tube. Some paintings look as if they were done with a brush. Perhaps they were painted with pads of fur, chewed twigs, or feathers.

Do these paintings have any meaning?

Yes. More than 100 painted caves have now been discovered in Europe. Some of the most beautiful paintings are found in the caves of Altamira in Spain and Lascaux in France. These paintings have been explained in many different ways. Perhaps we'll never know exactly why they were done and what the images meant to the artists. Fortunately in Australia and southern Africa, tens of thousands of paintings have been discovered. There is good evidence to show that what these artists painted was connected to their religious beliefs.

Why are Venus figurines fat?

We don't know. Some of the most fascinating prehistoric works of art are the fat little female statues called Venus figurines. More than 60 have been found. They were made between 27 000 and 20 000 years ago. Most look pregnant especially the Venus of Willendorf. Scientists think that they were symbols of a mother goddess. Her job was probably to make sure that the women had babies and that the men hunted successfully.

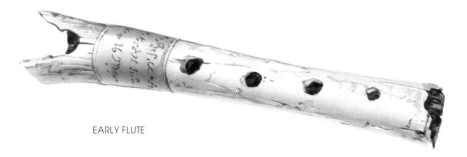

EARLY FLUTE

VENUS OF WILLENDORF

Did you know?

The earliest musical instrument was probably a flute. It is not certain when people first showed an interest in music. They may have sung songs long before they had musical instruments. One of the earliest musical instruments is the flute. This flute has been made from the bone of a bird and is 25 000 years old. Many birds have hollow bones with thin walls to make them light enough to fly. This was probably why the bone was chosen by the prehistoric flute-maker.

Do we have a future?

Of all the many kinds of creatures that have lived on Earth, the human species has been one of the last to evolve. We have also been the most successful because we are the only species that collects information and passes it on to the next generation. Because of this we do not adapt to nature any longer. We now change the environment to suit ourselves. Unfortunately this has upset the delicate balance of nature and many animals and plants have died out. Scientists are warning us that we must stop destroying the world because it is the only one we have. If we kill the world we too will become extinct.

What happened to the prairie?

It was destroyed by farming. On the great North American grasslands called prairies, prehistoric man lived in harmony with nature. Once farming was invented and the human population started to grow, these grasslands were ploughed under and used to plant crops. Today the animals and plants have almost disappeared and the prairie supports only one species: man.

Why is Africa turning into a desert?

Because of farming. The great African grasslands called savannahs used to support a large number of grazers (grass eaters) and browsers (leaf eaters). They lived in harmony because they did not compete with one another. People started to use the savannah for cattle farming but the cattle destroyed the natural ground cover. Droughts are a normal part of the African climate and when these happen the trampled ground is eroded and turned into a desert.

Should we practise birth control?

Yes. The best way to save the Earth and ourselves is to have fewer people on Earth. We can do this if everybody agrees to support birth control. A smaller human population will not exploit nature so much and there will be more food and shelter for everybody. This is a very sensitive issue, on which politicians and religious leaders are unlikely to agree.

Why is plankton important?

Because it produces most of our oxygen. A lot of the plankton in the sea is made up of tiny plants. They make their own food with the help of sunlight. This is called photosynthesis and is one of the most important processes on Earth. Through photosynthesis the plankton in the sea produces most of the oxygen we breathe. This is why we should not kill off the plankton by polluting the sea with oil and chemical waste from factories.

Are there too many people on Earth?

Yes. In prehistoric times people were so scarce that they could not upset the balance of nature. Today about 5 000 million people live on Earth. The world population is growing so fast and killing off so many plants and animals that nature cannot keep up and so a great many species become extinct.

Why are the great rain forests important?

Because they work like huge air filters. The tropical rain forests remove toxic or poisonous gases from the air we breathe. They play a very important part in keeping the environment clean. This is why we should stop the destruction of the rain forests.

Will we leave the Earth to live somewhere else?

Probably not. Some people seem to think that when the Earth eventually becomes too polluted to support life, we would somehow be able to move everybody to another planet. This won't happen. It would be impossible to move all the people on Earth elsewhere. Even to move just some people would be impractical and too expensive. There is also no guarantee that we would be able to find a planet on which humans can survive. If we cannot keep our own planet clean and healthy we would probably pollute other planets as well. Our best bet is therefore to stay right where we are on good old mother Earth and simply learn to clean up the environment ourselves.

Index

Answers
1. *Paranthropus*
2. Handy Man
3. *Homo erectus*
4. *Australopithecus* (Taung child)
5. Neanderthal woman
6. Cave Bear
7. Giant Buffalo